COOKING CLASS
HOLIDAY
RECIPES
COOKBOOK

PUBLICATIONS INTERNATIONAL, LTD.

Recipe Development: Karen A. Levin, Elizabeth King

Photography: Sacco Productions Limited, Chicago

Pictured on the front cover *(clockwise from top left):* Roast Turkey with Pan Gravy *(page 30)*, Cranberry-Apple Chutney *(page 60)*, Bûche de Noël *(page 74)*, Sweet Potato Gratin *(page 50)* and Broccoli with Red Pepper and Shallots *(page 48)*.
Pictured on the inside front cover: Linzer Torte *(page 78)*.
Pictured on the back cover: Chicken Wellington *(page 36)*.

ISBN: 0-7853-0787-7

Manufactured in U.S.A.

8 7 6 5 4 3 2 1

CONTENTS

French-Style Pizza Bites (*page 10*)

Glazed Pork Tenderloin (*page 40*)

Gingerbread Bears (*page 84*)

Whether you plan on dazzling your family and friends with a spectacular holiday meal, or are simply bringing a scrumptious dessert or savory vegetable to another's home, *Cooking Class Holiday Recipes* has the dishes to make whatever you serve special. With our step-by-step directions and clear how-to photographs you're sure to prepare delicious and impressive dishes!

The following Menu Planning section has ideas on how to select recipes for a perfect meal. There are also menu suggestions for several holiday celebrations and entertaining styles.

MENU PLANNING

The following are some helpful pointers to keep in mind when you are selecting recipes for a menu for entertaining.

• If this is one of your first company meals, keep it on the small side. It is easier to cook and serve for eight to ten rather than twenty people.

• Do not invite more people than you can comfortably seat at your table. Guests may become uncomfortable if they are crowded at a table.

• Make sure you have enough serving dishes and utensils.

• Select the entrée first, then plan the other dishes around it.

• Not every item on the menu needs to be a showstopper. Select one or two involved recipes and let the remainder be easy-to-prepare or store-bought.

• Eye appeal is an important consideration when planning a meal. Select foods with a variety of colors. Green or orange vegetables, red cranberry relish or multi-colored salad all add visual interest. A monochromatic meal is not only visually uninteresting, but is usually perceived as less flavorful.

• Pick foods that offer a variety of textures. Crisp-tender broccoli, creamy mashed potatoes and crunchy fruit all complement the firm, chewy texture of meats.

• A balanced meal offers contrasting flavors. The tart flavor of cranberries with the mild flavor of turkey make a perfect contrast.

• Choose side dishes with different shapes and sizes. Whole berry cranberry relish served along with peas and Brussels sprouts would not offer as much interest to a meal as whole berry cranberry relish served along with broccoli spears and diagonally sliced carrots.

• Pick recipes that can be made ahead of time, such as the Honey Wheat Brown-and-Serve Rolls, Cranberry-Apple Chutney, Linzer Torte or Gingerbread Bears. This leaves you more time for your guests.

• Many guests like to contribute to the festivities by bringing a side dish, dessert, appetizer or wine. Be sure to have some recommendations ready so that if you are asked, you may offer suggestions that complement the rest of the meal.

• Not all entertaining requires a full meal. Consider inviting family and friends over for just desserts or light snacks.

• Review the recipes you plan to make, then prepare a comprehensive grocery list. Those last minute dashes to the supermarket can be very stressful.

• Lastly, remember to serve hot foods hot and cold foods cold. For food safety, do not let any foods remain at room temperature for over 2 hours.

MENUS

To get you started, here is a selection of menus consisting of the delicious recipes found in this publication. Use them as a jumping off point, making substitutions as necessary to suite your personal tastes.

Traditional Turkey Dinner
Mixed Greens with Raspberry Vinaigrette
Roast Turkey with Pan Gravy
Sausage-Cornbread Stuffing
Sweet Potato Gratin
Cranberry-Apple Chutney
Buttery Mashed Potatoes
Brussels Sprouts in Mustard Sauce
Praline Pumpkin Tart
or *Bûche de Noël*

Hanukkah Celebration
Brisket of Beef
Challah
Orange-Glazed Carrots
Potato Latkes with applesauce
Rugelach

Calorie-Watcher's Feast

Three Mushroom Ratatouille
Butternut Bisque
Glazed Pork Tenderloin
Low-Calorie Mashed Potatoes
Broccoli with Red Pepper and Shallots
Individual Orange Soufflés

Contemporary Holiday Supper

Butternut Bisque
Chicken Wellington
Sesame-Onion Twists
Broccoli with Red Pepper and Shallots
Rich Chocolate Truffle Cake
Viennese Coffee

Heavenly Dessert Buffet

Bûche de Noël
or Praline Pumpkin Tart
Rich Chocolate Truffle Cake
Gingerbread Bears
Linzer Torte

Bites and Drinks

Pesto-Cheese Logs
Cheese & Sausage Bundles
French-Style Pizza Bites
Three Mushroom Ratatouille
Champagne Punch
Cranberry Sangría

CARVING

Once the menu has been planned, one of the more formidable tasks when preparing a large meal is carving the roast or bird. To help you carve the main attraction like a pro, follow these helpful guidelines and illustrations.

General Guidelines

• Allow enough time before serving not only for cooking the meat, but for stand time and carving.

• A stand time of 10 to 20 minutes is recommended for large cuts of meat, such as roasts, turkeys and whole chickens. Stand time allows the meat to finish cooking. Meat is easier to carve after standing. If meat is carved immediately out of the oven, it loses more of its flavorful juices.

• The temperatures given for removing meat and poultry from the oven are 5° to 10°F lower than the standard final temperatures. This is because the temperature continues to rise during the stand time.

• During the stand time, put the finishing touches on the salad and side dishes. This is also a good time to make the gravy.

• Unless you are planning on carving at the table, place the meat on a large cutting board with a well at one end to hold the juice. (Or, place a cutting board inside a baking sheet. The juice will collect in the baking sheet.) Use a long, sharp carving knife to slice the meat and a long-handled meat fork to steady the meat.

• While you are actually carving the meat, warm the bread in the oven.

Boneless Roasts

Use these directions for carving the following recipes: Roast Leg of Lamb (*page 42*) and Glazed Pork Tenderloin (*page 40*). The Glazed Pork Tenderloin may also be carved as directed for Brisket of Beef.

Boneless beef, pork and lamb roasts are easy to carve. Hold the roast steady with a long-handled meat fork. With the knife held perpendicular to the cutting board, cut across the grain into thin uniform slices. Cut the slices between 1/4 to 1/2 inch thick.

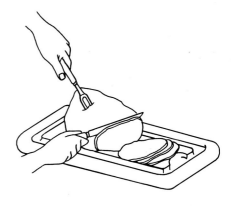

Use these directions for carving Brisket of Beef (*page 38*). A beef brisket is a thinner cut of meat. Follow the preceding directions, but slice the meat diagonally across the grain. This will give you a slice of meat with a larger surface area.

Standing Beef Rib Roast

Use these directions for carving Prime Rib with Yorkshire Pudding and Horseradish Cream Sauce (*page 33*).

For added stability, cut a wedge-shaped slice from the large end of the roast so that the meat will sit flat on the cutting board.

Insert a long-handled meat fork below the top rib. Slice across the top of roast toward the rib bone. This roast can be sliced between 1/2 to 3/4 inch thick.

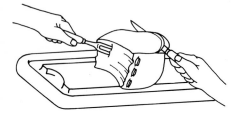

With the tip of the knife, cut along the rib bone to release the slice of meat.

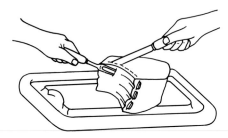

To remove the meat slice, slide the knife blade under the cut slice of meat. Holding it steady with a meat fork, lift the slice and place it on a platter.

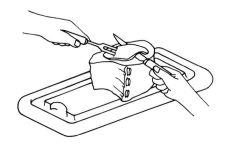

Bone-in Leg of Lamb

Use these directions for carving the bone-in variation for Roast Leg of Lamb (*page 42*).

For stability, place the roast on its side on the cutting board with the shank bone facing away from you. Cut two or three lengthwise slices from the section of the meat facing you. This will allow the meat to sit flat on the cutting board.

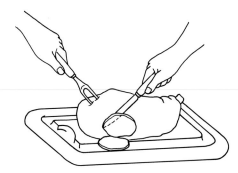

Turn the roast up so that it sits on the cut area. Hold the roast steady with a long-handled meat fork inserted into the meat opposite the shank bone. Holding the knife perpendicular to the cutting board and starting by the shank bone, cut across the grain into uniform, thin slices. Cut the slices between 1/4 to 1/2 inch thick.

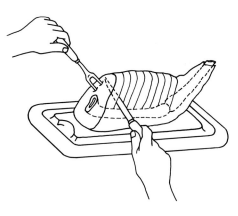

When you reach the aitch bone, release the slices by cutting under them along the leg bone.

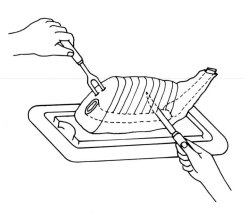

Roast Turkey

Use these directions for carving Roast Turkey with Pan Gravy (*page 30*).

To remove the leg, hold the drumstick and cut the skin with a carving knife between the thigh and the body to the joint. Pull the leg away from the body; cut through the joint at the backbone.

At this point, the drumstick may be served as it is or cut into slices. To slice the drumstick, hold the drumstick at an angle, bony side up. Cut down into ¹/₄-inch slices. Rotate the drumstick as you cut. Remove and discard the large tendons.

To remove the wings, insert a long-handled meat fork into the turkey to hold it steady. Cut down between the wing and the body of the turkey with a carving knife. Pull the wing out and cut through the joint.

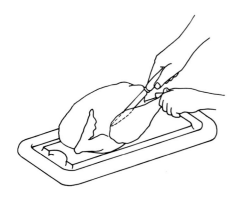

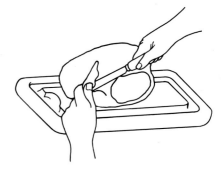

To separate the drumstick from the thigh, place the leg skin side up. Cut through at the joint.

To cut the thigh into slices, turn the thigh skin side down. Cut along the length of the bone, then turn skin side up and cut the meat across the grain.

To remove the breast meat, insert a long-handled meat fork into the turkey to hold it steady. At the base of the breast meat, make a horizontal cut across the breast to the bone. Cut the slices with straight even strokes down to the horizontal cut. At that point, the slices will fall free.

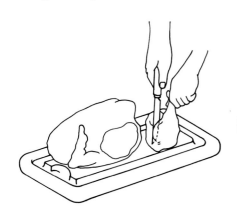

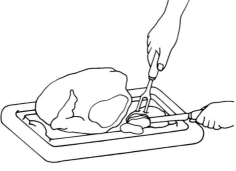

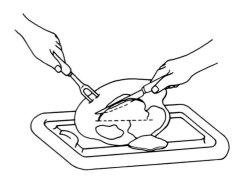

French-Style Pizza Bites (Pissaladière)

2 tablespoons olive oil
1 medium onion, thinly sliced
1 medium sweet red pepper, cut into 3-inch-long strips
2 cloves garlic, minced (technique on page 65)
⅓ cup pitted ripe olives, each cut into thin wedges
1 can (10 ounces) refrigerated pizza crust dough
¾ cup (3 ounces) finely shredded Swiss or Gruyère cheese

1. Position oven rack to lowest position. Preheat oven to 425°F. Grease large baking sheet; set aside.

2. Heat oil until hot in medium skillet over medium heat. Add onion, pepper and garlic. Cook and stir 5 minutes until vegetables are crisp-tender. Stir in olives. Remove from heat; set aside.

3. Remove dough from can and pat into 16 × 12-inch rectangle on prepared baking sheet.

4. Arrange vegetables over dough rectangle. Sprinkle with cheese. Bake 10 minutes. With long spatula, loosen crust from baking sheet. Slide crust onto oven rack. Bake 3 to 5 minutes more until golden brown.

5. Slide baking sheet under crust to remove crust from rack. Transfer to cutting board. Cut dough crosswise into eight 1¾-inch-wide strips. Cut dough diagonally into ten 2-inch-wide strips, making diamond pieces. Serve immediately. *Makes about 24 servings (2 diamonds per serving)*

Step 3. Patting dough into 16×12-inch rectangle on baking sheet.

Step 4. Sliding crust onto oven rack.

Step 5. Cutting dough into diamond-shaped pieces.

Coconut Fish Bites

1 cup flaked coconut
½ cup unsalted peanuts
1 egg
1 tablespoon soy sauce
¼ teaspoon salt
⅓ cup cornstarch
1 pound firm white fish (orange
    roughy, haddock or cod fish),
    cut into 1-inch pieces
Dipping Sauce (recipe follows)
1 quart vegetable oil for deep
    frying
Lemon wedges and fresh celery
    leaves for garnish

1. Place coconut and peanuts in food processor. Process using on/off pulsing action until peanuts are ground, but not pasty.

2. Blend egg, soy sauce and salt in pie plate. Place cornstarch and coconut mixture on separate pieces of waxed paper.

3. Toss fish cubes in cornstarch until well coated. Add to egg mixture; toss until coated with egg mixture. Lightly coat with coconut mixture. Refrigerate until ready to cook. Prepare Dipping Sauce; set aside.

4. Heat oil in heavy 3-quart saucepan over medium heat until deep-fat thermometer registers 365°F. Fry fish, in batches, 4 to 5 minutes or until golden brown and fish cubes flake easily when tested with fork. Adjust heat to maintain temperature. (Allow oil to return to 365°F between batches.) Drain on paper towels. Serve with Dipping Sauce. Garnish, if desired. *Makes about 24 appetizers*

Step 1. Ground coconut and peanut mixture.

Step 4. Frying fish.

Dipping Sauce

1 can (8 ounces) sliced peaches, undrained
2 tablespoons packed brown sugar
2 tablespoons ketchup
1 tablespoon vinegar
1 tablespoon soy sauce
2 teaspoons cornstarch

Combine all ingredients in food processor. Process until peaches are chopped. Bring mixture to a boil in 1-quart saucepan over medium heat; boil 1 minute until thickened, stirring constantly. Pour into serving bowl. (Sauce can be served warm or cold.)

Makes about 1¼ cups

Three Mushroom Ratatouille *(Calorie Watcher)*

1 package (3½ ounces) fresh
  shiitake mushrooms*
1 small tomato
  Fresh parsley
1 tablespoon olive oil
1 large onion, chopped
  (technique on page 60)
4 cloves garlic, minced
  (technique on page 65)
1 package (8 ounces) button
  mushrooms, chopped
1 package (6 ounces) crimini
  mushrooms, chopped
1 cup chicken broth
2 tablespoons grated Parmesan
  cheese
3 pita breads (6 inches *each*)
  Italian parsley for garnish

*Or, substitute 1 ounce dried black
Chinese mushrooms. Place dried
mushrooms in small bowl; cover with
warm water. Soak 20 minutes to soften.
Drain; squeeze out excess moisture.
Prepare as directed in step 1.

Nutritional information per serving *(3 pita
triangles with 1 tablespoon ratatouille on
each triangle):*

Calories	67
Protein	3 g
Fat	2 g
Saturated Fat	0 g
Carbohydrates	10 g
Cholesterol	1 mg
Sodium	195 mg

1. Remove stems from shiitake mushrooms; discard stems. Chop caps with utility knife.

2. Cut tomato into halves. Remove stem. Scrape out seeds with spoon. Chop enough tomato into small pieces with chef's knife to measure ½ cup.

3. To chop fresh parsley, place parsley in 1-cup measuring cup. Snip enough parsley with kitchen scissors to measure 2 tablespoons. Set aside.

4. Preheat broiler. Heat oil in large skillet over medium heat until hot. Add onion and garlic. Cook 5 minutes, stirring occasionally. Add all 3 types of mushrooms. Cook 5 minutes more, stirring often.

5. Add chicken broth. Bring to a boil. Cook about 10 minutes or until liquid is absorbed. Remove from heat. Stir in tomato, chopped parsley and cheese. Spoon into bowl.

6. Meanwhile, split each pita bread horizontally in half. Stack halves; cut the stack into 6 wedges. Arrange wedges in single layer on baking sheet. Broil 4 inches from heat 1 to 3 minutes or until wedges are toasted.

7. Arrange toasted pita bread triangles and warm dip in basket. Garnish, if desired.

Makes about 2¼ cups

Step 1. Chopping mushroom caps.

Step 3. Snipping parsley with scissors.

Butternut Bisque (Calorie Watcher)

1 medium butternut squash
(about 1½ pounds)
1 teaspoon margarine or butter
1 large onion, coarsely chopped
(1 cup) (technique on
page 60)
2 cans (about 14 ounces *each*)
reduced-sodium or regular
chicken broth, divided
½ teaspoon ground nutmeg or
freshly grated nutmeg*
⅛ teaspoon ground white pepper
Plain nonfat yogurt and chives
for garnish

*Whole nutmeg may be finely grated
using a nutmeg grater or mill.

Nutritional information per serving:

Calories	62
Protein	2 g
Fat	1 g
Saturated Fat	0 g
Carbohydrates	13 g
Cholesterol	30 mg
Sodium	841 mg

1. Remove skin from squash with vegetable peeler. Cut squash lengthwise in half with chef's knife; discard seeds. Cut flesh into ½-inch pieces; set aside.

2. Melt margarine in large saucepan over medium heat until foamy. Add onion. Cook and stir 3 minutes.

3. Add 1 can broth and squash. Bring to a boil over high heat. Reduce heat to low. Cover and simmer 20 minutes until squash is very tender.

4. Process squash mixture, in 2 batches, in food processor until smooth.

5. Return soup to saucepan; add remaining can of broth, nutmeg and pepper. Simmer, uncovered, 5 minutes, stirring occasionally.

6. At this point, the soup may be covered and refrigerated up to 2 days before serving. Reheat in large saucepan over medium heat until hot, stirring occasionally.

7. Ladle into soup bowls. Place yogurt in pastry bag fitted with round decorating tip. Pipe onto soup in decorative design. Garnish with chives, if desired.
Makes about 5 cups, 6 servings

Cream of Butternut Soup: Add ½ cup heavy cream or half-and-half with broth in step 5. Proceed as directed.

*Grating whole nutmeg with nutmeg grater.

Step 1. Peeling butternut squash.

Step 4. Processing squash mixture until smooth.

Cheese & Sausage Bundles

Salsa (recipe follows)
1/4 pound bulk hot Italian pork
    sausage
1 cup (4 ounces) shredded
    Monterey Jack cheese
1 can chopped green chili
    peppers, drained on paper
    towels
2 tablespoons finely chopped
    green onion
40 wonton wrappers
1 quart vegetable oil for deep
    frying

1. Prepare Salsa; set aside and keep warm. Brown sausage in small skillet over medium-high heat 6 to 8 minutes, stirring to separate meat. Drain drippings.

2. Combine sausage, cheese, peppers and onion in medium bowl. Spoon 1 round teaspoon sausage mixture near 1 corner of wonton wrapper. Brush opposite corner with water. Fold over corner; roll up jelly-roll style.

3. Moisten ends of roll with water. Bring ends together to make a "bundle," overlapping ends slightly; firmly press to seal. Repeat with remaining filling and wonton wrappers.

4. Heat oil in heavy 3-quart saucepan over medium heat until deep-fat thermometer registers 365°F. Fry bundles, a few at a time, about 1½ minutes or until golden. Adjust heat to maintain temperature. (Allow oil to return to 365°F between batches.) Drain on paper towels. Serve with Salsa. *Makes 40 appetizers*

Step 2. Rolling up wonton wrapper jelly-roll style.

Step 3. Bringing ends together to form a bundle.

Salsa

1 can (16 ounces) whole tomatoes, undrained
2 tablespoons olive oil
2 tablespoons chopped green onion
2 cloves garlic, minced (technique on
    page 65)
3 tablespoons chopped cilantro or parsley
    (technique on page 14)

Combine tomatoes with juice and oil in food processor; process until chopped. Pour into 1-quart saucepan. Stir in green onion and garlic. Bring to a boil over medium heat. Cook, uncovered, 5 minutes. Remove from heat. Stir in cilantro. *Makes 1³/4 cups*

Pesto-Cheese Logs

⅓ cup walnuts
1 package (8 ounces) cream
  cheese, softened
⅓ cup refrigerated pesto sauce
  (about half of 7-ounce
  package)
2 ounces feta cheese, crumbled
  (about ⅓ cup)
2 teaspoons cracked black
  pepper
2 tablespoons finely shredded
  carrot
2 tablespoons chopped fresh
  parsley (technique on
  page 14)
  Assorted crackers
  Carrot slivers, parsley and
  fresh thyme for garnish

1. Preheat oven to 350°F. To toast walnuts, spread in single layer on baking sheet. Bake 8 to 10 minutes or until golden brown, stirring frequently. Remove walnuts from sheet and cool.

2. Place walnuts in food processor. Process using on/off pulsing action until walnuts are ground, but not pasty. Remove from food processor; set aside.

3. Place cream cheese, pesto sauce and feta cheese in food processor. Process until cheese mixture is smooth.

4. Spread ¾ cup cheese mixture on sheet of waxed paper and form 4-inch-long log. Wrap waxed paper around cheese mixture. Repeat with remaining cheese mixture.

5. Refrigerate logs, at least 4 hours, until well chilled. Roll each chilled log back and forth to form 5-inch log.

6. Combine walnuts and black pepper on 1 sheet of waxed paper. Unwrap 1 log and roll it in nut mixture to coat.

7. Combine shredded carrot and parsley on another sheet of waxed paper. Unwrap remaining log and roll in carrot mixture to coat.

8. Serve immediately or wrap and refrigerate up to a day before serving. To serve, thinly slice log and serve with crackers. Garnish, if desired.   *Makes 2 logs*

Note: If you prefer, you may coat each log with ¼ cup chopped parsley instead of the walnuts, pepper and carrot.

Step 2. Ground nuts.

Step 5. Rolling chilled log back and forth to form 5-inch log.

Step 6. Rolling log in walnut-pepper mixture.

Viennese Coffee

1 cup heavy cream, divided
1 teaspoon powdered sugar
1 bar (3 ounces) bittersweet or
   semisweet chocolate
3 cups strong freshly brewed hot
   coffee
¼ cup crème de cacao or Irish
   cream (optional)
   Reserved chocolate shavings for
   garnish

1. Chill bowl, beaters and cream before whipping. Place ⅔ cup cream and sugar into chilled bowl. Beat with electric mixer at high speed until soft peaks form. To test, lift beaters from mixture; mixture should have droopy, but definite peaks. *Do not overbeat.*

2. Cover and refrigerate up to 8 hours. If mixture has separated slightly after refrigeration, whisk lightly with a wire whisk before using.

3. To make chocolate shavings for garnish, place waxed paper under chocolate. Holding chocolate in one hand, make short, quick strokes across chocolate with vegetable peeler; set aside. Break remaining chocolate into pieces.

4. Place remaining ⅓ cup cream in heavy, small saucepan. Bring to a simmer over medium-low heat. Add chocolate pieces; cover and remove from heat. Let stand 5 minutes or until chocolate is melted; stir until smooth.

5. Add hot coffee to chocolate mixture. Heat on low heat just until bubbles form around the edge of pan and coffee is heated through, stirring frequently. Remove from heat; stir in crème de cacao.

6. Pour into 4 warmed mugs. Top with whipped cream. Garnish with chocolate shavings.   *Makes about 3½ cups, 4 servings*

Step 1. Testing whipped cream mixture for soft peaks.

Step 3. Making chocolate shavings.

Step 5. Heating coffee mixture.

Hot Mulled Cider

1 orange
1 lemon
12 whole cloves
6 cups apple cider
⅓ cup sugar
3 cinnamon sticks
12 whole allspice berries
Additional cinnamon sticks and
citrus strips for garnish

1. Pierce 6 evenly spaced holes around orange and lemon with point of wooden skewer.

2. Insert whole cloves into the holes.

3. Cut a slice out of the orange to include all of the cloves. Cut the remainder of orange into thin slices with utility knife. Repeat procedure with lemon.

4. Combine orange slices, lemon slices, cider, sugar, 3 cinnamon sticks and allspice in medium saucepan. Bring just to a simmer over medium heat. *Do not boil.* Reduce heat to low; cook 5 minutes.

5. Pour cider through strainer into mugs. Discard fruit and seasonings. Garnish, if desired.   *Makes 6 cups, 6 servings*

Step 1. Piercing orange with wooden skewer.

Step 2. Inserting whole cloves into orange.

Step 5. Pouring cider through strainer into mug.

Cranberry Sangría

1 orange
1 lime
1 bottle (750 ml) Beaujolais or
    dry red wine
1 cup cranberry juice cocktail
1 cup orange juice
½ cup cranberry-flavored liqueur
    (optional)

*Orange and lime may be scored before slicing to add a special touch. To score, make a lengthwise groove in fruit with citrus stripper. Continue to make grooves ¼ to ½ inch apart until entire fruit has been grooved.

1. Cut orange and lime into thin slices with utility knife.

2. Combine orange slices, lime slices, wine, cranberry juice cocktail, orange juice and liqueur in large glass pitcher. Chill 2 to 8 hours before serving.

3. Pour into glasses; add orange and/or lime slices from the sangría to each glass.

Makes about 7 cups, 10 to 12 servings

Sparkling Sangría: Just before serving, tilt pitcher and slowly add 2 cups well-chilled sparkling water or club soda. Pour into glasses; add orange and/or lime slices from sangría to each glass. Makes about 9 cups, 12 to 15 servings.

Step 1. Cutting lime into thin slices.

Step 3. Adding orange and lime slices to glass.

Sparkling Sangría: Slowly pouring sparkling water into Cranberry Sangría.

Champagne Punch

1 orange
1 lemon
¼ cup cranberry-flavored liqueur
    or cognac
¼ cup orange-flavored liqueur or
    triple sec
1 bottle (750 ml) pink or regular
    champagne or sparkling
    white wine, well chilled
    Fresh cranberries (optional)
    Citrus strips for garnish

1. Remove colored peel, not white pith, from orange and lemon with citrus stripper or vegetable peeler in long thin strips. Refrigerate orange and lemon for another use.

2. Combine peels, cranberry-flavored and orange-flavored liqueurs in glass pitcher. Cover and chill 2 to 6 hours.

3. Just before serving, tilt pitcher to one side and slowly pour in champagne. Leave peels in pitcher for added flavor.

4. Place a cranberry in the bottom of each glass. Pour into champagne glasses. Garnish with citrus strips tied into knots, if desired.

Makes 4 cups, 6 to 8 servings

Nonalcoholic Cranberry Punch: Pour 3 cups well-chilled club soda into ⅔ cup (6 ounces) cranberry cocktail concentrate, thawed. Makes 3½ cups, 6 servings.

Step 1. Removing orange peel with citrus stripper.

Step 3. Slowly pouring champagne into pitcher.

Roast Turkey with Pan Gravy

1 **fresh or thawed frozen turkey (12 to 14 pounds),* reserve giblets and neck (discard liver or reserve for another use)**
   Sausage-Cornbread Stuffing (page 62) or your favorite stuffing (optional)
2 **cloves garlic, minced (technique on page 65) (optional)**
½ **cup butter, melted**
   Turkey Broth with Giblets (page 32)
1 **cup dry white wine or vermouth**
3 **tablespoons all-purpose flour**
   Salt and freshly ground black pepper

*A 12- to 14-pound turkey should take 2 to 3 days to thaw in the refrigerator. *Do not thaw at room temperature.*

1. Preheat oven to 450°F. Rinse turkey; pat dry with paper towels.

2. Prepare stuffing, if desired.

3. Stuff body and neck cavities loosely with stuffing, if desired.

4. Fold skin over openings and close with skewers. Tie legs together with cotton string or tuck through skin flap, if provided. Tuck wings under turkey.

5. Place turkey on meat rack in shallow roasting pan. If desired, stir garlic into butter. Insert meat thermometer in thickest part of thigh not touching bone. Brush ⅓ of butter mixture evenly over turkey.

6. Place turkey in oven and immediately turn temperature down to 325°F. Roast 18 to 20 minutes per pound for unstuffed turkey or 22 to 24 minutes per pound for stuffed turkey, brushing with butter mixture after 1 hour and then after 1½ hours. Baste with pan juices every hour of roasting. (Total roasting time should be 4 to 5 hours.) If turkey is overbrowning, tent with foil. Turkey is done when internal temperature reaches 180°F and legs move easily in sockets.

7. While turkey is roasting, prepare Turkey Broth with Giblets.

continued on page 32

Step 4. Tucking wings under turkey.

Step 5. Inserting meat thermometer.

Step 6. Basting turkey with pan juices.

Roast Turkey with Pan Gravy,
continued

8. Transfer turkey to cutting board; tent with foil. Let stand 15 minutes while preparing gravy.

9. Pour off and reserve all juices from roasting pan. To deglaze the pan, pour wine into pan. Place over burners and cook over medium-high heat, scraping up browned bits and stirring constantly 2 to 3 minutes or until the mixture has reduced by about half.

10. Spoon off ⅓ cup fat from pan drippings;** discard any remaining fat. Place ⅓ cup fat in large saucepan.

11. Add flour; cook over medium heat 1 minute, stirring constantly. Slowly stir in the 3 cups Turkey Broth, the defatted turkey drippings from the roasting pan and the deglazed wine mixture from the roasting pan.

12. Cook over medium heat 10 minutes, stirring occasionally. Stir in reserved chopped giblets; heat through. Season with salt and pepper to taste.

13. Carve turkey with carving knife. (Techniques on page 9.)
Makes 12 servings and 3½ cups gravy

**Or, substitute ⅓ cup butter or margarine for turkey fat.

Creamy Turkey Gravy: Stir in 1 cup heavy cream with giblets; proceed as directed in step 12. Makes 4½ cups gravy.

Turkey Broth with Giblets

Reserved giblets and neck from turkey (discard liver or reserve for another use)
4 **cups water**
1 **can (about 14 ounces) chicken broth**
1 **medium onion, cut into quarters**
2 **medium carrots, coarsely chopped or sliced**
4 **large parsley sprigs**
1 **bay leaf**
1 **teaspoon dried thyme leaves, crushed**
10 **whole black peppercorns**

1. For broth, combine turkey giblets and neck, water and chicken broth in 3-quart saucepan. Bring to a boil over high heat; skim off any foam.

2. Stir in onion, carrots, parsley, bay leaf, thyme and peppercorns. Reduce heat to low. Simmer, uncovered, 1½ to 2 hours, stirring occasionally. (If liquid evaporates too quickly, add additional ½ cup water.) Cool to room temperature.

3. Strain broth; set aside. If broth measures less than 3 cups, add water to equal 3 cups liquid. If broth measures more than 3 cups, bring to a boil and heat until liquid is reduced to 3 cups.

4. Remove meat from neck and chop giblets finely; set aside.

5. Broth may be prepared up to 1 day before serving. Cover giblets and broth separately and refrigerate.
Makes 3 cups

Step 9. Deglazing pan.

Step 10. Spooning off ⅓ cup fat from drippings.

Turkey Broth with Giblets: Step 3. Straining broth.

Prime Rib with Yorkshire Pudding and Horseradish Cream Sauce

3 cloves garlic, minced (technique on page 65)
1 teaspoon freshly ground black pepper
1 (3-rib) standing beef roast, trimmed* (about 6 to 7 pounds)
Yorkshire Pudding (page 34)
Horseradish Cream Sauce (page 34)

*Ask meat retailer to remove the chine bone for easier carving. Fat should be trimmed to ¼-inch thickness.

1. Preheat oven to 450°F. Combine garlic and pepper; rub over surfaces of roast.

2. Place roast, bone side down, (the bones take the place of a meat rack) in shallow roasting pan. Insert meat thermometer in thickest part of roast, not touching bone or fat. Roast 15 minutes.

3. Reduce oven temperature to 325°F. Roast 20 minutes per pound or until internal temperature is 120° to 130°F for rare, 135° to 145°F for medium.

4. Meanwhile, prepare Yorkshire Pudding and Horseradish Cream Sauce.

5. When roast has reached desired temperature, transfer to cutting board; tent with foil. Let stand in warm place 20 to 30 minutes to allow for easier carving. Temperature of roast will continue to rise about 10°F during stand time.

6. Reserve ¼ cup drippings from roasting pan. Immediately after roast has been removed from oven, increase oven temperature to 450°F.

7. While pudding is baking, carve roast with carving knife. (Techniques on pages 7-8.) Serve with Yorkshire Pudding and Horseradish Cream Sauce.

Makes 6 to 8 servings

continued on page 34

Step 2. Inserting meat thermometer.

Step 5. Tenting roast with foil during stand time.

Step 6. Reserving ¼ cup drippings.

Prime Rib with Yorkshire Pudding and Horseradish Cream Sauce, continued

Yorkshire Pudding

1 **cup milk**
2 **eggs**
½ **teaspoon salt**
1 **cup all-purpose flour**
¼ **cup reserved drippings from roast or unsalted butter**

1. Process milk, eggs and salt in food processor or blender 15 seconds. Add flour; process 2 minutes. Let batter stand in food processor at room temperature 30 minutes to 1 hour. (This lets the flour fully absorb liquid for a more tender pudding.)

2. Place drippings in 9-inch square baking pan. Place in 450°F oven 5 minutes. (Use oven mitt when removing pan from oven as pan will be very hot.)

3. Process batter another 10 seconds; pour into hot drippings. *Do not stir.*

4. Immediately return pan to oven. Bake 20 minutes. Reduce oven temperature to 350°F; bake 10 minutes until pudding is golden brown and puffed. Cut into squares.

Makes 6 to 8 servings

Horseradish Cream Sauce

1 **cup heavy cream**
⅓ **cup prepared horseradish, undrained**
2 **teaspoons balsamic or red wine vinegar**
1 **teaspoon dry mustard**
¼ **teaspoon sugar**
⅛ **teaspoon salt**

1. Chill large bowl, beaters and cream before whipping. Pour cream into chilled bowl and beat with electric mixer at high speed until soft peaks form. To test, lift beaters from cream; mixture should have droopy, but definite peaks. *Do not overbeat.*

2. Combine horseradish, vinegar, mustard, sugar and salt in medium bowl.

3. Fold whipped cream into horseradish mixture by gently cutting down to bottom of bowl, scraping up side of bowl, then folding over top of mixture. Repeat until whipped cream is evenly incorporated into horseradish mixture. Cover and refrigerate at least 1 hour. Sauce may be made up to 8 hours before serving. *Makes 1½ cups*

Yorkshire Pudding: Step 3. Pouring batter into hot drippings.

Horseradish Cream Sauce: Step 1. Testing whipped cream mixture for soft peaks.

Chicken Wellington

6 large boneless skinless chicken
    breast halves (about 6 ounces
    each)
¾ teaspoon salt, divided
¼ teaspoon freshly ground black
    pepper, divided
¼ cup butter or margarine,
    divided
12 ounces mushrooms (button or
    crimini), finely chopped
½ cup finely chopped shallots or
    onion (technique on page 48)
2 tablespoons port wine or
    cognac
1 tablespoon fresh thyme leaves
    or 1 teaspoon dried thyme
    leaves, crushed
1 package (17¼ ounces) frozen
    puff pastry, thawed
1 egg, separated*
1 tablespoon country-style
    Dijon-style mustard
1 teaspoon milk

*To separate eggs, see page 74, steps 2
and 3.

1. Sprinkle chicken with ¼ teaspoon salt and ⅛ teaspoon pepper. Melt 2 tablespoons butter in skillet over medium heat. Cook 3 chicken breasts 3 minutes; turn over. Cook 3 minutes more until golden brown. (Center will be springy to the touch.) Transfer to plate. Cook remaining chicken; cool slightly.

2. Melt remaining 2 tablespoons butter in skillet over medium heat. Add mushrooms and shallots. Cook and stir 5 minutes or until mushrooms release their liquid. Add wine, thyme, remaining ½ teaspoon salt and ⅛ teaspoon pepper; simmer 10 minutes or until liquid evaporates, stirring often. Cool.

3. Roll out each pastry sheet to 15 × 12-inch rectangle. Cut each into 3 (12 × 5-inch) rectangles. Cut small amount of pastry from corners to use as decoration, if desired.

4. Beat egg white in cup; brush over pastry rectangles. Place 1 cooled chicken breast on one side of each pastry rectangle. Spread ½ teaspoon mustard over each chicken breast, then spread with ¼ cup mushroom mixture.

5. Fold pastry over chicken. Fold edge of bottom dough over top; press edges to seal. Place on *ungreased* baking sheet.

6. Beat yolk with milk. Brush over pastry; decorate with pastry scraps, if desired. Brush decorations. Cover loosely with plastic wrap. Refrigerate until cold 1 to 4 hours.

7. Preheat oven to 400°F. Remove plastic wrap. Bake chicken 25 to 30 minutes or until deep golden brown and chicken is 160°F. Garnish, if desired.   *Makes 6 servings*

Step 4. Spreading mushroom mixture over chicken.

Step 5. Pressing edges of dough together to seal.

Step 6. Decorating with pastry scraps.

Brisket of Beef

1 whole well-trimmed beef
   brisket (about 5 pounds)
4 cloves garlic, minced (technique
   on page 65)
½ teaspoon freshly ground black
   pepper
2 large onions, peeled and cut
   into ¼-inch slices
1 bottle (12 ounces) chili sauce
¾ cup beef broth, beer or water
2 tablespoons Worcestershire
   sauce
1 tablespoon packed brown sugar

1. Preheat oven to 350°F. Place brisket, fat side up, in shallow roasting pan. Spread garlic evenly over brisket; sprinkle with pepper.

2. Separate onions into rings; arrange over brisket. Combine chili sauce, broth, Worcestershire sauce and sugar; pour over brisket and onions.

3. Cover with heavy-duty foil or roasting pan lid.

4. Roast 2 hours. Turn brisket over; stir onions into sauce and spoon over brisket. Cover; roast 1 to 2 hours more or until fork-tender. (The roasting time depends on thickness of brisket and quality of meat.)

5. Transfer brisket to cutting board. Tent with foil; let stand 10 minutes.

6. At this point, the brisket may be covered and refrigerated up to 1 day before serving. To reheat brisket, cut diagonally into thin slices with carving knife. Place brisket slices and juice in large skillet. Cover and heat over medium-low heat until heated through.

7. Stir juices in roasting pan. Spoon off and discard fat from juices. (Juices may be thinned to desired consistency with water or thickened by simmering, uncovered, in saucepan.)

8. Carve brisket across grain into thin slices with carving knife. (Technique on page 7.) Spoon juices over brisket.

Makes 10 to 12 servings

Variation: If desired, stir red boiling potatoes, cut carrots, parsnips or turnips into juices during last hour of cooking time.

Step 1. Spreading garlic over brisket.

Step 2. Pouring chili sauce mixture over brisket.

Step 3. Covering pan with heavy-duty foil.

Glazed Pork Tenderloin *(Calorie Watcher)*

2 whole well-trimmed pork tenderloins (about 1½ pounds *each*)
½ cup currant jelly or canned jellied cranberry sauce
1 tablespoon bottled grated horseradish, drained
½ cup chicken broth
¼ cup Rhine or other sweet white wine
Salt and pepper to taste (optional)

Nutritional information per serving:

Calories	229
Protein	25 g
Fat	5 g
Saturated Fat	1 g
Carbohydrates	19 g
Cholesterol	81 mg
Sodium	208 mg

1. Preheat oven to 325°F. Place tenderloins on meat rack in shallow roasting pan.

2. Combine jelly and horseradish in microwavable dish or small saucepan. Heat at HIGH 1 minute or over low heat on rangetop until jelly is melted; stir well.

3. Brush half of mixture over tenderloins.

4. Roast 30 minutes; turn tenderloins over. Brush with remaining jelly mixture. Continue to roast 30 to 40 minutes depending on thickness of tenderloins or until thermometer registers 160°F.* Remove thermometer and check temperature of other tenderloin.

5. Transfer tenderloins to cutting board; tent with foil. Let stand 10 minutes.

6. Remove meat rack from roasting pan. To deglaze the pan, pour broth and wine into pan. Place over burners and cook over medium-high heat, stirring frequently and scraping up any browned bits, 4 to 5 minutes or until sauce is reduced to ½ cup.

7. Strain sauce through a fine-mesh strainer; season to taste with salt and pepper.

8. Carve tenderloins into thin slices with carving knife. (Technique on page 7.) Serve with sauce.   *Makes 6 servings*

*Since pork tenderloins are so thin, the most accurate way to measure internal temperature is with an instant read thermometer, which has a narrower stem than a standard meat thermometer. Insert thermometer into thickest part of tenderloin. Do not leave the thermometer in the tenderloin during roasting since the thermometer is not ovenproof.

Step 6. Deglazing pan.

Step 7. Pouring sauce through strainer.

Roast Leg of Lamb

3 tablespoons coarse-grained
  mustard
2 cloves garlic, minced*
  (technique on page 65)
1½ teaspoons rosemary leaves,
  crushed
½ teaspoon freshly ground black
  pepper
1 leg of lamb, well-trimmed,
  boned, rolled and tied (about
  4 pounds)
  Mint jelly (optional)

*For a more intense garlic flavor inside
the meat, cut garlic into slivers. Cut small
pockets at random intervals throughout
roast with tip of sharp knife; insert garlic
slivers.

1. Preheat oven to 400°F. Combine mustard, garlic, rosemary and pepper. Rub mustard mixture over surface of lamb. At this point lamb may be covered and refrigerated up to 24 hours before roasting.

2. Place roast on meat rack in shallow foil-lined roasting pan. Insert meat thermometer in thickest part of roast.

3. Roast 15 minutes. *Reduce oven temperature to 325°F; roast 20 minutes per pound until roast registers 150°F for medium.*

4. Transfer roast to cutting board; tent with foil. Let stand 10 minutes before carving. Temperature of roast will continue to rise 5° to 10°F during stand time.

5. Cut strings with scissors; discard. Carve roast into thin slices with carving knife. (Technique on page 7.) Serve with mint jelly, if desired. *Makes 6 to 8 servings*

Bone-in Roast Leg of Lamb: Prepare as directed above, except roast a 5- to 6-pound bone-in leg of lamb 25 minutes per pound. After stand time, carve roast into thin slices with carving knife. (Techniques on page 8.)

*Inserting garlic slivers into lamb.

Step 1. Rubbing mustard mixture over lamb.

Step 2. Inserting meat thermometer.

Orange-Glazed Carrots

Fresh ginger (optional)
1 pound fresh or frozen baby
carrots, thawed
⅓ cup orange marmalade
2 tablespoons butter
2 teaspoons Dijon-style mustard

1. Peel small piece of fresh ginger with vegetable peeler or sharp knife. Grate enough ginger with ginger grater or finest side of box-shaped grater to measure ½ teaspoon. Set aside.

2. To cook carrots, heat 1 inch lightly salted water in 2-quart saucepan over high heat to a boil. Immediately add carrots. Return to a boil. Reduce heat to low. Cover and simmer 10 to 12 minutes for fresh carrots (8 to 10 minutes for frozen carrots) or until crisp-tender.

3. Drain well; return carrots to pan.

4. Stir in marmalade, butter, mustard and ginger. Simmer, uncovered, over medium heat 3 minutes until carrots are glazed, stirring occasionally.

5. At this point, carrots may be transferred to a microwavable casserole dish with lid. Cover and refrigerate up to 8 hours before serving. To reheat, microwave at HIGH 4 to 5 minutes or until hot.   *Makes 6 servings*

Note: Recipe may be doubled to serve 10 to 12.

Step 1. Grating fresh ginger with ginger grater.

Step 2. Testing doneness.

Step 4. Stirring in remaining ingredients.

Brussels Sprouts in Mustard Sauce

1½ **pounds fresh Brussels sprouts***
1 **tablespoon butter or margarine**
⅓ **cup chopped shallots or onion**
⅓ **cup half-and-half**
1½ **tablespoons tarragon Dijon-style mustard** or **Düsseldorf mustard**
¼ **teaspoon salt**
⅛ **teaspoon freshly ground black pepper** *or* **ground nutmeg**
1½ **tablespoons grated Parmesan cheese (optional)**

*Or, substitute 2 (10-ounce) packages frozen Brussels sprouts for fresh Brussels sprouts. Omit steps 1, 2 and 3. Cook according to package directions; drain and rinse as directed in step 4.

**Or, substitute 1½ tablespoons Dijon-style mustard *plus* ½ teaspoon dry tarragon leaves, crushed, for tarragon Dijon-style mustard.

1. Cut stem from each Brussels sprout and pull off outer bruised leaves.

2. For faster, more even cooking, cross-hatch core by cutting an "X" deep into the stem end of each Brussels sprout with paring knife. If some Brussels sprouts are larger than others, cut large Brussels sprouts lengthwise into halves.

3. Use a large enough saucepan to allow Brussels sprouts to fit in a single layer. Bring 2 quarts salted water to a boil in saucepan. Add Brussels sprouts; return to a boil. Boil, uncovered, 7 to 10 minutes or until almost tender when pierced with fork.

4. Drain in colander. Rinse under cold water to stop cooking; drain thoroughly.

5. Melt butter in same saucepan over medium heat until foamy. Add shallots; cook 3 minutes, stirring occasionally. Add half-and-half, mustard, salt and pepper. Simmer 1 minute until thickened.

6. Add drained Brussels sprouts; heat about 1 minute or until heated through, tossing gently with sauce.

7. At this point, Brussels sprouts may be covered and refrigerated up to 8 hours before serving. Reheat in saucepan over low heat. Or, place in microwavable covered dish and reheat in microwave oven at HIGH about 3 minutes until hot.

8. Just before serving, sprinkle with cheese, if desired. *Makes 4 cups, 6 to 8 servings*

Step 1. Pulling off outer bruised leaves.

Step 2. Cutting an "X" in stem end of Brussels sprouts.

Broccoli with Red Pepper and Shallots *(Calorie Watcher)*

2 bunches fresh broccoli (about 2¼ pounds)
1 large red bell pepper
3 large shallots (3 ounces) or 1 small onion
2 teaspoons margarine or butter
½ teaspoon salt
¼ teaspoon freshly ground black pepper
¼ cup sliced almonds, toasted* (optional)

*To toast almonds, see toasting walnuts directions on page 20, step 1.

Nutritional information per 1 cup serving:

Calories	73
Protein	6 g
Fat	2 g
Saturated Fat	0 g
Carbohydrates	12 g
Cholesterol	0 mg
Sodium	239 mg

1. Trim leaves from broccoli stalks. Trim ends of stalks. Cut broccoli into flowerets by removing the heads to include a small piece of stem. Peel stalks, then cut into 1-inch pieces.

2. To cook broccoli, heat 2 quarts lightly salted water in 3-quart saucepan over high heat to a boil. Immediately add broccoli. Return to a boil. Boil, uncovered, 3 to 5 minutes until bright green and tender. Drain broccoli in colander. Rinse under cold water; drain thoroughly.

3. Rinse bell pepper under cold running water. To seed pepper, stand on end on cutting board. Cut off sides in 3 to 4 lengthwise slices with utility knife. (Cut close to, but not through stem.) Discard stem and seeds. Scrape out any remaining seeds. Rinse inside of pepper under cold running water, then cut into short thin strips.

4. Remove papery outer skin from shallots. Cut off root end. Cut shallots into thin slices.

5. At this point, vegetables may be wrapped separately and refrigerated up to 6 hours before cooking.

6. Melt margarine in 12-inch nonstick skillet over medium heat. Add bell pepper and shallots. Cook 3 minutes, stirring occasionally. Add broccoli to skillet. Cook 4 to 6 minutes, stirring occasionally. Sprinkle with salt and black pepper; mix well. Garnish with almonds, if desired.

Makes 6 cups, 6 to 8 servings

Step 1. Cutting broccoli stalks into 1-inch pieces.

Step 3. Cutting sides from pepper.

Step 4. Cutting root end from shallot.

Sweet Potato Gratin

3 pounds sweet potatoes (about 5 large)
½ cup butter or margarine, divided
¼ cup *plus* 2 tablespoons packed light brown sugar, divided
2 eggs
⅔ cup orange juice
2 teaspoons ground cinnamon, divided
½ teaspoon salt
¼ teaspoon ground nutmeg
⅓ cup all-purpose flour
¼ cup uncooked old-fashioned oats
⅓ cup chopped pecans or walnuts

1. Bake sweet potatoes until tender in preheated 350°F oven 1 hour. Or, pierce sweet potatoes several times with fork and place on microwavable plate. Microwave at HIGH 16 to 18 minutes, rotating and turning over sweet potatoes after 9 minutes. Let stand 5 minutes.

2. While sweet potatoes are hot, cut lengthwise into halves. Scrape hot pulp from skins into large bowl.

3. Beat ¼ cup butter and 2 tablespoons sugar into sweet potatoes with electric mixer at medium speed until butter is melted. Beat in eggs, orange juice, 1½ teaspoons cinnamon, salt and nutmeg, scraping down side of bowl once. Beat until smooth. Pour mixture into 1½-quart baking dish or gratin dish, smoothing top.

4. For topping, combine flour, oats, remaining ¼ cup sugar and remaining ½ teaspoon cinnamon in medium bowl. Cut in remaining ¼ cup butter with pastry blender or 2 knives until mixture becomes coarse crumbs. Stir in pecans.

5. Sprinkle topping evenly over sweet potatoes.

6. At this point, Sweet Potato Gratin may be covered and refrigerated up to 1 day. Let stand at room temperature 1 hour before baking.

7. Preheat oven to 350°F.

8. Bake 25 to 30 minutes or until sweet potatoes are heated through. For a crisper topping, broil 5 inches from heat 2 to 3 minutes or until golden brown.

Makes 6 to 8 servings

Step 2. Scraping sweet potatoes from skins into bowl.

Step 3. Beating sweet potato mixture until smooth.

Step 4. Cutting butter into topping mixture.

Potato Latkes

2 large or 3 medium baking
    (russet) potatoes (about
    1¾ pounds)
1 large onion (8 ounces)
2 eggs
¼ cup matzo meal
¾ teaspoon salt
¼ teaspoon freshly ground black
    pepper
2 tablespoons vegetable oil,
    divided
  Applesauce (optional)
  Sour cream (optional)

1. To prepare potatoes, remove skins with vegetable peeler.

2. Shred potatoes and onion with shredding disc of food processor or shred by hand using a box-shaped grater.

3. Place potato mixture in large bowl. Add eggs, matzo meal, salt and pepper; mix well.

4. Heat 1 tablespoon oil in large nonstick skillet over medium-low heat until hot. Drop potato mixture by level ¼ cupfuls into skillet.

5. Use back of spatula to flatten potato mixture into 3½-inch patties, about ½ inch thick.

6. Cook about 4 minutes per side or until golden brown. Transfer to ovenproof platter lined with paper towels.

7. Keep warm in 200°F oven while preparing remaining latkes. Add remaining 1 tablespoon oil as needed. Serve warm with applesauce or sour cream. Garnish as desired.

Makes about 18 latkes

Step 2. Shredding potatoes in food processor.

Step 4. Dropping potato mixture by ¼ cupfuls into hot oil mixture.

Step 5. Flattening potato mixture into patties with back of spatula.

Low-Calorie Mashed Potatoes (Calorie Watcher)

2 pounds medium red boiling potatoes
4 large cloves garlic, peeled
¾ cup cultured buttermilk (1½% fat)
½ teaspoon salt
¼ teaspoon freshly ground black pepper
2 tablespoons chopped chives for garnish

Nutritional information per ½ cup:

Calories	110
Protein	3 g
Fat	0 g
Saturated Fat	0 g
Carbohydrates	25 g
Cholesterol	1 mg
Sodium	162 mg

1. To prepare potatoes, remove skins with vegetable peeler. Cut into chunks.

2. Place potatoes and garlic in large saucepan. Add enough water to cover; bring to a boil over high heat. Reduce heat to medium. Simmer, uncovered, 20 to 30 minutes or until potatoes are fork-tender; drain.

3. Place potatoes and garlic in medium bowl. Mash with potato masher or beat with electric mixer at medium speed until smooth.* Add buttermilk, salt and pepper. Stir with fork until just combined. Garnish, if desired.

Makes 4 cups, 8 servings

*For a smoother texture, force potatoes through potato ricer or food mill into medium bowl. Finish as directed in step 3.

Buttery Mashed Potatoes: Follow directions given above. In step 3, add 1 tablespoon butter or margarine to potatoes along with buttermilk, salt and pepper.

Step 1. Cutting potatoes into chunks.

Step 2. Placing potatoes in saucepan.

*Forcing potatoes through ricer.

Mixed Greens with Raspberry Vinaigrette

½ cup walnut pieces
1 shallot
⅓ cup vegetable oil
2½ tablespoons raspberry vinegar
½ teaspoon salt
½ teaspoon sugar
  Romaine lettuce leaves
  Spinach leaves
  Red leaf lettuce leaves
1 cup red seedless grapes, halved

1. Preheat oven to 350°F. To toast walnuts, spread in single layer on baking sheet. Bake 6 to 8 minutes or until lightly golden brown, stirring frequently. Remove walnuts from baking sheet and cool. Coarsely chop with chef's knife; set aside.

2. Remove papery outer skin from shallot. Cut off root end. Finely chop enough shallot with chef's knife to measure 1 tablespoon.

3. Place oil, vinegar, shallot, salt and sugar in small bowl or small jar with lid. Whisk together or cover and shake jar until mixed. Cover; refrigerate up to 1 week.

4. Wash greens separately in several changes of cold water. Drain well and if necessary pat with paper towels to remove excess moisture. Or, spin in salad spinner to remove moisture.

5. Discard any wilted or bruised leaves. Cut or tear off stems if they are woody.

6. Tear enough romaine lettuce into bite-sized pieces to measure 2 packed cups. Tear enough spinach into bite-sized pieces to measure 2 packed cups. Tear enough red leaf lettuce into bite-sized pieces to measure 2 packed cups.

7. Combine greens, grapes and cooled walnuts in large bowl. Just before serving, add dressing; toss well to coat.

Makes 6 to 8 servings

Step 2. Cutting root end from shallot.

Step 4. Placing greens in salad spinner.

Step 6. Packing romaine lettuce into measuring cup.

Winter Pear and Stilton Salad

1/3 cup extra virgin olive oil
1 1/2 tablespoons sherry wine vinegar or white wine vinegar
1 tablespoon Dijon-style mustard
4 teaspoons honey
1/4 teaspoon salt
3 ounces assorted gourmet mixed salad greens, such as oakleaf, frisee, watercress, radicchio, arugula or escarole
1 1/2 ounces Boston or bibb lettuce leaves
2 ripe Bosc, Bartlett or Anjou pears
Lemon juice
6 ounces Stilton or Gorgonzola cheese
Freshly ground black pepper

1. Place oil, vinegar, mustard, honey and salt in small bowl. Whisk together until combined. Cover and refrigerate up to 2 days.

2. Wash greens in several changes of cold water. Drain well and if necessary pat with paper towels to remove excess moisture. Or, spin in salad spinner to remove moisture.

3. Discard any wilted or bruised leaves. Cut or tear off stems if they are woody.

4. Tear enough assorted gourmet mixed greens into bite-sized pieces to measure 5 packed cups. Tear enough Boston lettuce into bite-sized pieces to measure 2 packed cups.

5. Cut pears into quarters with utility knife. Remove stems and core. Cut each quarter into 1/2-inch pieces. To help prevent discoloration, brush pear pieces with lemon juice, if desired.

6. Crumble enough cheese with fingers to measure 1 1/2 cups.

7. Combine all salad greens in large bowl. Add pears, cheese and dressing. Toss lightly to coat; sprinkle with pepper.

Makes 6 to 8 servings

Step 2. Washing greens.

Step 4. Packing lettuce into measuring cup.

Step 6. Crumbling cheese.

Cranberry-Apple Chutney

1 package (12 ounces) fresh or
   frozen cranberries (about
   3½ cups)
2 medium Granny Smith apples
1 medium onion
1¼ cups granulated sugar
½ cup water
½ cup golden raisins
½ cup packed light brown sugar
¼ cup cider vinegar
1 teaspoon ground cinnamon
1 teaspoon ground ginger
⅛ teaspoon ground cloves
⅛ teaspoon ground allspice
½ cup walnuts or pecans, toasted*
   and chopped (optional)

*To toast walnuts, see directions on page 20, step 1.

1. Wash cranberries and pick through, discarding any stems or withered cranberries.

2. Peel apples with vegetable peeler. Cut into quarters; remove stems and core with sharp knife. Cut apples into ¼-inch pieces. Cut enough to make 2 cups.

3. To chop onion, peel skin. Cut onion in half through root with utility knife. Place cut side down on cutting board. Holding knife horizontally, make cuts parallel to board, almost to root end. Next, cut onion vertically into thin slices, holding onion with fingers to keep its shape, then turn onion and cut crosswise to root end. (The closer the cuts are, the finer the onion is chopped.) Repeat with remaining onion half.

4. Combine granulated sugar and water in heavy 2-quart saucepan. Cook over high heat until boiling. Boil gently 3 minutes.

5. Add cranberries, apples, onion, raisins, brown sugar, vinegar, cinnamon, ginger, cloves and allspice. Bring to a boil over high heat. Reduce heat to medium. Simmer, uncovered, 20 to 25 minutes or until mixture is very thick, stirring occasionally. Cool; stir in walnuts.

6. Cover and refrigerate up to 2 weeks before serving.

Makes about 3½ cups without walnuts or 4 cups with walnuts

Note: This chutney makes a wonderful appetizer when spooned over cream cheese spread on melba rounds.

Step 2. Cutting apples into ¼-inch pieces.

Step 3. Chopping onion.

Sausage-Cornbread Stuffing

1 recipe day-old Cornbread*
   (page 64)
2 medium onions
2 cloves garlic
8 ounces bulk pork sausage
   (regular or spicy)
½ cup butter or margarine
2 teaspoons dried sage
1 teaspoon poultry seasoning
¾ to 1¼ cups chicken broth
   Sage leaves for garnish

*Or, substitute 1 package (16 ounces)
prepared dry cornbread crumbs for
homemade cornbread. Omit step 1.

1. Preheat oven to 350°F. Crumble cornbread coarsely. Crumble enough to make 6 cups. Spread evenly in 15 × 10-inch jelly-roll pan. Bake 20 to 25 minutes or until dry.

2. To chop onions, peel skin. Cut onions in half through root with utility knife. Place cut side down on cutting board. Holding knife horizontally, make cuts parallel to board, almost to root end. Next, cut onion vertically into thin slices, holding onion with finger to keep its shape, then turn onion and cut crosswise to root end. (The closer the cuts are, the finer the onion is chopped.) Repeat with remaining onion halves.

3. To mince garlic, trim ends of garlic cloves. Slightly crush cloves under flat side of chef's knife blade; peel away skin. Chop garlic with chef's knife until garlic is in uniform fine pieces. Set aside.

4. Brown sausage in large skillet over medium-high heat until no longer pink, stirring to crumble meat. Drain sausage on paper towels; set aside. Wipe skillet with paper towels to remove grease.

5. Melt butter in same skillet over medium heat until foamy. Cook onions and garlic in butter 10 minutes until onions are softened. Stir in sage and poultry seasoning; cook 1 minute more.

continued on page 64

Step 1. Spreading cornbread crumbs in pan.

Step 2. Chopping onion.

Step 4. Stirring sausage to crumble.

Sausage-Cornbread Stuffing, continued

6. Combine cornbread crumbs, sausage and onion mixture in large bowl.

7. ***If stuffing is to be cooked in a turkey,*** drizzle ¾ cup broth over stuffing; toss lightly until evenly moistened. Stuff body and neck cavities loosely with stuffing. Stuffing may be prepared up to 1 day before using. Do not stuff the turkey until just before you are ready to roast it. Roast according to directions given on page 30 or according to instructions given with turkey.

8. ***If stuffing is to be cooked separately,*** drizzle 1¼ cups broth over stuffing; toss stuffing lightly until evenly moistened. Transfer to 3-quart casserole.

9. At this point, Sausage-Cornbread Stuffing may be covered and refrigerated up to 1 day before baking.

10. Preheat oven to 350°F.

11. Bake 45 minutes (55 to 60 minutes if refrigerated) or until heated through. For a drier stuffing, uncover during last 15 minutes of baking. Garnish, if desired.   *Makes 12 cups stuffing*

Cornbread

1¼ **cups yellow cornmeal**
 ¾ **cup all-purpose flour**
 2 **tablespoons sugar**
 1 **tablespoon baking powder**
 ¾ **teaspoon salt**
 1 **egg**
 1 **cup milk**
 3 **tablespoons butter or margarine, melted and cooled**

1. Preheat oven to 425°F. Grease 9-inch square baking pan; set aside.

2. Combine cornmeal, flour, sugar, baking powder and salt in medium bowl. Combine egg, milk and butter in 4-cup measure; add to cornmeal mixture. Stir just until dry ingredients are moistened. Pour into prepared pan.

3. Bake 20 to 25 minutes or until golden brown and wooden toothpick inserted in center comes out clean. Cool completely on wire rack.

4. Cornbread may be prepared up to 2 days before using as stuffing. Cover; let stand at room temperature.
          Makes 6 cups cornbread crumbs

Step 7. Stuffing turkey.

Cornbread: Step 2. Adding milk mixture to dry ingredients.

Cornbread: Step 3. Testing doneness of cornbread with wooden toothpick.

Wild Rice Mushroom Stuffing

½ cup uncooked wild rice
6 ounces fresh mushrooms*
1 large onion
1 clove garlic
 Day-old French bread (about 4 ounces)
½ cup butter or margarine
½ teaspoon rubbed sage
½ teaspoon dried thyme leaves, crushed
½ teaspoon salt
¼ teaspoon freshly ground black pepper
1 cup chicken broth
½ cup coarsely chopped pecans
 Thyme sprigs for garnish

*Or, substitute 1½ cups fresh sliced shiitake mushroom caps for 3 ounces fresh mushrooms.

1. Rinse and cook rice according to package directions; set aside.

2. Wipe mushrooms clean with damp paper towel. Cut thin piece from stem; discard. With paring knife, cut mushrooms into slices to measure 3 cups.

3. To chop onion, peel skin. Cut onion in half through root with utility knife. Place cut side down on cutting board. Holding knife horizontally, make cuts parallel to board, almost to root end. Next, cut onion vertically into thin slices, holding onion with fingers to keep its shape, then turn onion and cut crosswise to root end. (The closer the cuts are, the finer the onion is chopped.) Repeat with remaining onion half.

4. To mince garlic, trim ends of garlic clove. Slightly crush clove under flat side of chef's knife blade; peel away skin. Chop garlic with chef's knife until garlic is in uniform fine pieces. Set aside.

continued on page 66

Step 2. Wiping mushroom with damp paper towel.

Step 3. Chopping onion.

Step 4. Crushing garlic to remove skin.

Wild Rice Mushroom Stuffing,
continued

5. Cut French bread with a serrated knife into ½-inch slices. Stack a few of the slices. Cut lengthwise into ½-inch-wide strips, then cut crosswise to form ½-inch cubes. Cut enough bread to measure 4 cups.

6. Spread bread cubes in single layer on baking sheet. Broil 5 to 6 inches from heat 4 minutes or until lightly toasted, stirring after 2 minutes; set aside.

7. Heat butter in large skillet over medium heat until foamy. Add onion and garlic. Cook and stir 3 minutes. Add mushrooms; cook 3 minutes, stirring occasionally. Add sage, ½ teaspoon thyme, salt and pepper. Add cooked rice; cook 2 minutes, stirring occasionally. Stir in broth. Add pecans and toasted bread cubes; toss lightly.

8. Transfer to 1½-quart casserole.

9. At this point, Wild Rice Mushroom Stuffing may be covered and refrigerated up to 8 hours before baking.

10. Preheat oven to 325°F.

11. Cover with casserole lid or foil. Bake 40 minutes (50 minutes if refrigerated) or until heated through. Garnish, if desired.

Makes 6 to 8 servings

Step 5. Cutting French bread into cubes.

Step 6. Spreading bread cubes on baking sheet.

Step 7. Tossing bread cubes with broth mixture.

Praline Pumpkin Tart

1¼ cups all-purpose flour
1 tablespoon granulated sugar
¾ teaspoon salt, divided
¼ cup vegetable shortening
¼ cup butter or margarine
3 to 4 tablespoons cold water
1 can (16 ounces) pumpkin
1 can (13 ounces) evaporated
   milk (1½ cups)
2 eggs
⅔ cup packed brown sugar
1 teaspoon ground cinnamon
½ teaspoon ground ginger
¼ teaspoon ground cloves
   Praline Topping (page 70)
   Sweetened Whipped Cream
     (page 72)
   Additional cinnamon and
     pecans halves for garnish

1. For crust, combine flour, granulated sugar and ¼ teaspoon salt in large bowl. Cut in shortening and butter using pastry blender or 2 knives until mixture forms pea-sized pieces.

2. Sprinkle flour mixture with water, 1 tablespoon at a time. Toss with fork until mixture holds together. Press together to form ball. Wrap in plastic wrap. Refrigerate about 1 hour or until chilled.

3. Remove plastic wrap from dough. Flatten dough into 5- to 6-inch disc. Lightly flour surface and rolling pin. Roll dough in short strokes starting in the middle of the disc rolling out toward the edge with rolling pin. Rotate dough ¼ turn to the right. Sprinkle more flour under dough and on rolling pin as necessary to prevent sticking. Continue to roll and rotate dough 2 to 3 more times. Roll out dough to ⅛-inch thickness.

4. Trim dough to 1 inch larger than inverted 10-inch tart pan with removable bottom or 1½ inches larger than inverted 9-inch pie plate. Place rolling pin on one side of dough. Gently roll dough over rolling pin once.

5. Carefully lift rolling pin and dough, unrolling dough over tart pan. Ease dough into tart pan with fingertips. Do not stretch dough. Cut dough even with edge of tart pan. (Roll and flute edge of dough in pie plate.)

6. Cover tart crust with plastic wrap and refrigerate 30 minutes to relax dough.

7. Preheat oven to 400°F.

continued on page 70

Step 3. Rolling out dough.

Step 4. Rolling dough over rolling pin.

Step 5. Unrolling dough over tart pan.

Praline Pumpkin Tart, continued

8. To blind bake tart crust, pierce tart crust with tines of fork at ¼-inch intervals, about 40 times.

9. Cut a square of foil about 4 inches larger than tart pan. Line tart pan with foil. Fill with dried beans, uncooked rice or ceramic pie weights.

10. Bake 10 minutes or until set. Remove from oven. Gently remove foil lining and beans. Return to oven and bake 5 minutes or until very light brown. Cool completely on wire rack. (If using beans or rice, save to use again for blind baking. The beans or rice are no longer usable in recipes.)

11. For filling, preheat oven to 400°F. Beat pumpkin, milk, eggs, brown sugar, 1 teaspoon cinnamon, remaining ½ teaspoon salt, ginger and cloves in large bowl with electric mixer at low speed. Pour into cooled tart crust. Bake 35 minutes.

12. Prepare Praline Topping. Sprinkle topping over center of tart leaving 1½-inch rim around edge of tart.

13. Bake 15 minutes more or until knife inserted 1 inch from center comes out clean.

14. Cool completely on wire rack. Prepare Sweetened Whipped Cream and spoon into decorating bag with fluted tip. Pipe whipped cream around edge of pie, making decorative edge. Sprinkle additional cinnamon over whipped cream. Garnish with pecan halves.

Makes 8 servings

Praline Topping

⅓ **cup packed brown sugar**
⅓ **cup chopped pecans**
⅓ **cup uncooked quick-cooking oats**
1 **tablespoon butter or margarine, softened**

Place sugar, pecans and oats in small bowl. Cut in butter with pastry blender or 2 knives until crumbs forms.

Step 8. Piercing crust with tines of fork.

Step 9. Filling foil liner with dried beans.

Step 13. Testing doneness with knife.

Rich Chocolate Truffle Cake

2 packages (8 ounces *each*)
    semisweet chocolate
    (16 squares)
1½ cups butter or margarine
1 cup sugar
½ cup light cream
6 large eggs
2 teaspoons vanilla
    Chocolate Curls (page 72)
    Chocolate Glaze (page 72)
    Sweetened Whipped Cream
    (page 72)
    Mint leaves for garnish

1. Preheat oven to 350°F. Line bottom of 9-inch springform pan with foil, tucking foil edges under bottom. Attach springform side. Bring foil up around side of pan. Grease foil-lined bottom and side of pan with butter; set aside.

2. Heat chocolate, butter, sugar and cream in heavy 2-quart saucepan over low heat until chocolate melts and mixture is smooth, stirring frequently. Remove from heat.

3. Beat eggs and vanilla in large bowl with wire whisk until frothy. Slowly whisk in warm chocolate mixture until well blended. *Do not vigorously beat mixture.* You do not want to incorporate air into the mixture.

4. Pour batter into prepared pan. Bake 45 minutes or until wooden toothpick inserted about 1 inch from edge comes out clean and center is set. Cool cake completely in pan on wire rack.

5. Prepare Chocolate Curls; refrigerate.

6. When cake is cool, carefully remove side of springform pan. Leave cake on bottom of pan. Wrap cake in foil. Refrigerate until well chilled, at least 4 hours or overnight.

7. Prepare Chocolate Glaze. Unwrap cake. Remove from bottom of pan and place upside-down on cake plate. Surround cake with waxed paper strips.

continued on page 72

Step 1. Lining bottom of pan with foil.

Step 4. Testing doneness of cake with wooden toothpick.

Step 7. Placing waxed paper strips around edge of plate.

Rich Chocolate Truffle Cake,
continued

8. Spread top and side of cake with warm glaze, using metal spatula. Remove waxed paper after glaze sets.

9. Prepare Sweetened Whipped Cream. Spoon cream mixture into decorating bag with medium star tube. Pipe cream around edge of cake.

10. Garnish piped cream with Chocolate Curls. Refrigerate until serving. Just before serving, garnish with mint leaves.

Makes 16 to 20 servings

Chocolate Curls

1 square (1-ounce) chocolate, coarsely chopped
1 teaspoon vegetable shortening

1. Place chocolate and shortening in 1-cup glass measure. Microwave at HIGH about 1 minute or until melted, stirring after 30 seconds of cooking.

2. Pour melted chocolate onto back of baking sheet, marble slab or other heat-resistant flat surface. Quickly spread chocolate into a very thin layer with metal spatula. Refrigerate about 10 minutes or until firm, but still pliable. (Technique on page 77.)

3. When chocolate is just firm, use small straight-edge metal spatula or paring knife. Holding spatula at a 45° angle, push spatula firmly along baking sheet, under chocolate, so chocolate curls as it is pushed. (Technique on page 77.) (If chocolate is too firm to curl, let stand a few minutes at room temperature. Refrigerate again if it becomes too soft.)

4. Using small skewer or toothpick, transfer curls to waxed paper. (Technique on page 77.) Store in cool, dry place until ready to use.

Chocolate Glaze

1 cup semisweet chocolate chips
2 tablespoons butter or margarine
3 tablespoons half-and-half
2 tablespoons light corn syrup

Heat chocolate chips and butter in heavy 1-quart saucepan over low heat, stirring frequently. Remove from heat. Stir in half-and-half and corn syrup until smooth. *Makes about 1¼ cups*

Sweetened Whipped Cream

1 cup heavy cream
2 tablespoons powdered sugar
½ teaspoon vanilla

Chill large bowl, beaters and cream before whipping. Place cream, sugar and vanilla into chilled bowl and beat with electric mixer at high speed until soft peaks form. To test, lift beaters from whipping cream; mixture should have droopy, but definite peaks. *Do not overbeat.* Refrigerate.

Makes about 2 cups

Step 9. Piping cream around edge of cake.

Sweetened Whipped Cream: Testing whipped cream mixture for soft peaks.

Bûche de Noël

5 eggs
¾ cup cake flour
½ teaspoon baking powder
½ teaspoon salt
1 cup granulated sugar, divided
1 teaspoon vanilla
½ cup powdered sugar
1 cup semisweet chocolate chips
¾ cup heavy cream
1 tablespoon rum
  Cocoa Frosting (page 77)
  White Chocolate Curls
    (page 77)
2 teaspoons unsweetened cocoa
    powder (optional)

1. Preheat oven to 375°F. Grease 15½×10½-inch jelly-roll pan; line pan with waxed paper. Grease again; set aside.

2. To separate egg white from yolk, gently tap egg in center against hard surface, such as side of bowl. Holding shell half in each hand, gently transfer yolk back and forth between 2 shell halves. Allow white to drip down between 2 shells into bowl.

3. When all white has dripped into bowl, place yolk in another bowl. Transfer white to third bowl. Repeat with remaining eggs. Egg whites must be free from any egg yolk to reach proper volume when beaten.

4. Place flour, baking powder and salt in small bowl; stir to combine.

5. Beat egg yolks and ⅔ cup granulated sugar in small bowl with electric mixer at high speed about 5 minutes or until thick and lemon colored, scraping down side of bowl once. Beat in vanilla; set aside.

6. Beat egg whites in clean large bowl using clean beaters with electric mixer at high speed until foamy. Gradually beat in remaining ⅓ cup granulated sugar, 1 tablespoon at a time, until stiff peaks form. After beaters are lifted from egg white mixture, stiff peaks should remain on surface, and when bowl is tilted, mixture will not slide around.

Step 2. Separating an egg white from an egg yolk.

Step 6. Testing egg white mixture for stiff peaks.

continued on page 76

Bûche de Noël, continued

7. Fold flour mixture into egg yolk mixture with rubber spatula by gently cutting down to bottom of bowl, scraping up side of bowl, then folding over top of mixture. Repeat until flour mixture is evenly incorporated into yolk mixture.

8. Fold flour mixture into egg white mixture, following technique described in step 7, until flour mixture is evenly incorporated into meringue.

9. Spread mixture into prepared pan. Bake 12 to 15 minutes or until cake springs back when lightly touched with finger. Meanwhile, lightly sift powdered sugar over clean dish towel.

10. Loosen warm cake from edges of pan with spatula; invert onto prepared towel. Remove pan; carefully peel off paper.

11. Gently roll up cake in towel from short end, jelly-roll style. Let cake cool completely on wire rack.

12. For chocolate filling, place chocolate chips and cream in heavy, 1-quart saucepan. Heat over low heat until chocolate is melted, stirring frequently. Pour into small bowl; stir in rum. Cover and refrigerate about 1½ hours or until filling is spreading consistency, stirring occasionally.

13. Prepare Cocoa Frosting; refrigerate until ready to use. Prepare White Chocolate Curls; refrigerate until ready to use.

14. Unroll cake; remove towel. Spread cake with chilled chocolate filling to within ½ inch of edge; reroll cake.

15. Spread Cocoa Frosting over cake roll. Garnish with White Chocolate Curls. Sprinkle with cocoa.

Makes 12 servings

Step 10. Inverting cake onto prepared towel.

Step 11. Gently rolling up cake in towel.

Step 14. Spreading unrolled cake with chocolate filling.

Cocoa Frosting

1 cup heavy cream
2 tablespoons unsweetened Dutch
    processed* cocoa powder, sifted
1/2 cup powdered sugar, sifted
1 teaspoon vanilla

*The Dutch processed or European-style cocoa gives this frosting an intense chocolate flavor and a rich color. Other unsweetened cocoas can be substituted, but the flavor may be milder and the color may be lighter.

Beat cream, cocoa, sugar and vanilla with electric mixer at medium speed until soft peaks form. To test, lift beaters from whipped cream; mixture should have droopy, but definite peaks. *Do not overbeat.* Refrigerate until ready to use. *Makes about 2 cups*

White Chocolate Curls

1 package (8 ounces) white chocolate,
    coarsely chopped
1 tablespoon vegetable shortening

1. Place white chocolate and shortening in 2-cup glass measure. Microwave at HIGH about 1 1/2 minutes or until melted, stirring after every 30 seconds of cooking.

2. Pour melted white chocolate onto back of baking sheet, marble slab or other heat-resistant flat surface. Quickly spread chocolate into a very thin layer with metal spatula. Refrigerate about 10 minutes or until firm, but still pliable.

3. When chocolate is just firm, use small straight-edge metal spatula or paring knife. Holding spatula at a 45° angle, push spatula firmly along baking sheet, under chocolate, so chocolate curls as it is pushed. (If chocolate is too firm to curl, let stand a few minutes at room temperature. Refrigerate again if it becomes too soft.)

4. Using small skewer or toothpick, transfer curls to waxed paper. Store in cool, dry place until ready to use.

White Chocolate Curls: Step 2. Spreading white chocolate on back of baking sheet.

White Chocolate Curls: Step 3. Forming curls.

White Chocolate Curls: Step 4. Transferring curls to waxed paper.

Linzer Torte

½ cup whole almonds, toasted*
1½ cups all-purpose flour
1 teaspoon ground cinnamon
¼ teaspoon salt
¾ cup granulated sugar
½ cup butter or margarine
½ teaspoon grated lemon peel
1 egg
¾ cup raspberry or apricot jam
Powdered sugar

*To toast almonds, see toasting walnuts directions page 20, step 1.

1. Place almonds in food processor. Process using on/off pulsing action until almonds are ground, but not pasty.

2. Preheat oven to 375°F.

3. Combine flour, almonds, cinnamon and salt in medium bowl; set aside.

4. Beat granulated sugar, butter and lemon peel in large bowl using electric mixer at medium speed about 5 minutes or until light and fluffy, scraping down side of bowl once. Beat in egg until well blended.

5. Beat in flour mixture at low speed until well blended. Spoon ⅔ of dough onto bottom of 10-inch tart pan with removable bottom. Pat dough evenly over bottom and up side of pan. Spread jam over bottom of dough.

6. Roll remaining ⅓ of dough on lightly floured surface with lightly floured rolling pin into 10×6-inch square. Cut dough into 10½-inch strips using a pizza wheel or sharp knife.

7. Arrange 4 to 5 strips of dough lengthwise across jam. Arrange another 4 to 5 strips of dough crosswise across top. Press ends of dough strips into edge of crust.

8. Bake 25 to 35 minutes or until crust is golden brown. Cool completely in pan on wire rack. Remove torte from pan. Cut into wedges. Sprinkle with powdered sugar.

9. Store, tightly covered, at room temperature 1 to 2 days. *Makes 12 servings*

Step 6. Cutting dough into strips with pizza cutter.

Step 7. Arranging strips in a lattice pattern on torte.

Individual Orange Soufflés *(Calorie Watcher)*

Nonstick cooking spray
3 oranges
1½ tablespoons cornstarch
3 tablespoons orange-flavored liqueur
6 egg whites
⅛ teaspoon salt
6 tablespoons granulated sugar
1½ tablespoons sliced almonds (optional)
1½ tablespoons powdered sugar (optional)

Nutritional information per serving:

Calories	101
Protein	3 g
Fat	0 g
Saturated Fat	0 g
Carbohydrates	21 g
Cholesterol	0 mg
Sodium	75 mg

1. Preheat oven to 450°F. Spray 6 individual soufflé dishes (8 to 10 ounces each) with cooking spray. Place dishes on jelly-roll pan; set aside.

2. Grate colored portion, not white pith, of orange peel using grater. Grate enough orange peel to equal 1½ teaspoons.

3. Cut peel and membrane from oranges; section oranges over 1-quart saucepan. Dice oranges. There will be 1½ cups juice and pulp.

4. Stir in cornstarch until smooth. Cook and stir over medium heat until mixture comes to a boil and thickens slightly. Remove from heat. Stir in liqueur and reserved orange peel.

5. Beat egg whites and salt with electric mixer at high speed in large bowl until soft peaks form. To test, lift beaters from egg whites; they should have droopy, but definite peaks.

6. Gradually beat in granulated sugar, 1 tablespoon at a time, until stiff peaks form and sugar is dissolved. After beaters are lifted from egg white mixture, stiff peaks should remain on surface, and when bowl is tilted, mixture will not slide around.

7. Fold ¼ of egg white mixture into orange mixture, using rubber spatula or wire whisk. Then, fold all of orange mixture into remaining egg white mixture. Spoon into prepared dishes. Sprinkle with almonds.

8. Immediately bake 12 to 15 minutes or until soufflés are puffed and browned. Sprinkle with powdered sugar. Serve immediately.

Makes 6 servings

Step 5. Testing egg white mixture for soft peaks.

Step 6. Testing egg white mixture for stiff peaks.

Step 7. Folding egg white mixture into orange mixture.

Rugelach

1½ cups all-purpose flour
¼ teaspoon salt
¼ teaspoon baking soda
½ cup butter or margarine
1 package (3 ounces) cream
    cheese, softened
⅓ cup *plus* ¼ cup granulated
    sugar, divided
1 teaspoon grated lemon peel,
    divided
1 cup ground toasted walnuts* or
    1 cup whole almonds
1 teaspoon ground cinnamon
2 tablespoons honey
1 tablespoon lemon juice
    Powdered sugar

*To grind walnuts, see directions on page 20, step 2.

1. Mix flour, salt and baking soda in bowl.

2. Beat butter, cream cheese, ⅓ cup granulated sugar and ½ teaspoon lemon peel in bowl with electric mixer at medium speed 5 minutes or until fluffy, scraping down bowl once.

3. Gradually add flour mixture. Beat at low speed until blended; scrape down bowl once.

4. Form dough into 3 (5-inch) discs; wrap in plastic wrap; refrigerate until firm, about 2 hours.

5. Preheat oven to 375°F. Grease 2 cookie sheets. Combine walnuts, remaining ¼ cup granulated sugar and cinnamon in medium bowl; set aside. Combine honey, remaining ½ teaspoon lemon peel and lemon juice in small bowl; set aside.

6. Working with 1 piece of dough at a time, unwrap and place dough on lightly floured surface. Roll out dough with lightly floured rolling pin to 10-inch circle. Keep remaining dough refrigerated.

7. Brush with ⅓ of honey mixture. Sprinkle with ⅓ of nut mixture. Lightly press nut mixture into dough.

8. Cut circle into 12 triangles with pizza cutter or sharp knife. Beginning with wide end of triangle, tightly roll up, jelly-roll style. Place cookies 1 inch apart on cookie sheets.

9. Repeat with 2 remaining dough pieces and filling ingredients. Bake 10 to 12 minutes or until lightly golden brown. Let cookies stand on cookie sheets 1 minute. Remove cookies to wire rack; cool completely. Sprinkle with powered sugar. Store tightly covered.

Makes 3 dozen

Step 6. Rolling out dough.

Step 7. Sprinkling nut mixture over dough.

Step 8. Rolling up dough jelly-roll style.

Gingerbread Bears

3½ cups all-purpose flour
2 teaspoons ground cinnamon
1½ teaspoons ground ginger
1 teaspoon salt
1 teaspoon baking soda
1 teaspoon ground allspice
1 cup butter or margarine,
    softened
1 cup firmly packed brown sugar
1 teaspoon vanilla
⅓ cup molasses
2 eggs
    Assorted cookie nonpareils and
        colored sugar (optional)
    Prepared creamy or gel-type
        frostings in tubes (optional)
    Assorted candies and grated
        chocolate (optional)

1. Mix flour, cinnamon, ginger, salt, baking soda and allspice in medium bowl.

2. Beat butter, sugar and vanilla in large bowl with electric mixer at medium speed about 5 minutes or until light and fluffy, scraping down side of bowl once. (Mixture will not be completely smooth.) Beat in molasses and eggs until blended, scraping down once.

3. Beat in flour mixture at low speed until well blended. Divide dough into 3 equal pieces. Flatten each piece of dough into a disc; wrap in plastic wrap. Refrigerate at least 2 hours.

4. Preheat oven to 350°F. Grease large cookie sheets.

5. Working with 1 piece of dough at a time, remove plastic wrap and place dough on lightly floured surface. Roll out dough with lightly floured rolling pin to ⅛-inch thickness. Keep remaining dough refrigerated.

6. Cut out dough with 3-inch bear-shaped cookie cutters. Place cookies 1 inch apart on prepared cookie sheets. Roll pieces of dough scraps into balls and ropes to make eyes, noses and to decorate bears. Decorate bears with nonpareils, if desired.

7. Bake 10 minutes or until bottoms of cookies are golden brown. Let stand on cookie sheet 1 minute. Remove cookies with spatula to wire rack; cool completely.

8. Pipe or spread frosting on cooled cookies to decorate. Decorate with assorted nonpareils, colored sugar, assorted candies and/or grated chocolate. Store tightly covered at room temperature.

Makes about 3½ dozen cookies

Step 5. Rolling out dough to ⅛-inch thickness.

Step 6. Cutting out dough with cookie cutters.

Step 8. Decorating cooled cookies.

Honey Wheat Brown-and-Serve Rolls

2 packages active dry yeast
1 teaspoon sugar
¾ cup warm water (105° to 115°F)
2 cups whole wheat flour
2 to 3 cups all-purpose flour, divided
¼ cup vegetable shortening
¼ cup honey
1 teaspoon salt
1 egg

1. To proof yeast, sprinkle yeast and sugar over warm water in small bowl; stir until yeast is dissolved. Let stand 5 minutes until mixture is bubbly.*

2. Combine whole wheat flour and 2 cups all-purpose flour in medium bowl. Measure 1½ cups flour mixture into large bowl. Add yeast mixture, shortening, honey, salt and egg. Beat with electric mixer at low speed until smooth, scraping down side of bowl once. Increase mixer speed to medium; beat 2 minutes, scraping down side of bowl once.

3. Reduce speed to low; beat in 1 cup flour mixture. Increase mixer speed to medium; beat 2 minutes, scraping down side of bowl once. Stir in remaining flour mixture and enough additional all-purpose flour (about ¼ cup) with wooden spoon to make a soft dough.

4. Turn dough out onto lightly floured surface; flatten slightly. To knead dough, fold dough in half toward you and press dough away from you with heels of hands. Give dough a quarter turn and continue folding, pushing and turning. Continue kneading 8 to 10 minutes or until smooth and elastic, adding more flour to prevent sticking, if necessary.

5. Shape dough into a ball; place in large greased bowl. Turn dough over so that top is greased. Cover with clean kitchen towel. Let rise in warm place (80° to 85°F) away from drafts, about 1½ hours or until doubled in bulk.

Step 1. Proofing yeast.

Step 4. Kneading dough.

continued on page 88

Honey Wheat Brown-and-Serve Rolls,
continued

6. To test dough, lightly press 2 fingertips about ½ inch into dough. Dough is ready if indentations remain when fingertips are removed.

7. Punch down dough by pushing down the center of dough with fist, then pushing edges of dough into center. Turn dough onto lightly floured surface. Knead dough several turns to remove all the large air bubbles; cover with towel for 15 minutes to let dough rest. Meanwhile, grease 24 muffin cups.

8. Divide dough into 24 pieces. Cut 1 piece into thirds. Roll each third into a ball. Place 3 balls in each muffin cup. Repeat with remaining dough. Cover with clean kitchen towel. Let rise in warm place away from drafts about 30 minutes until doubled in bulk.

9. Preheat oven to 275°F.**

10. Bake 20 to 25 minutes or until rolls are set but not brown. Immediately remove rolls from muffin cups and cool completely on wire racks. Store in resealable plastic food storage bags in refrigerator or freezer.

11. To bake rolls, thaw rolls if frozen. Preheat oven to 400°F. Grease large jelly-roll pan. Place rolls on jelly-roll pan. Bake 8 to 10 minutes or until golden brown.   *Makes 24 rolls*

*If yeast does not bubble, it is no longer active. Discard mixture and start over with new yeast. Always check expiration date on yeast package. Also, water that is too hot will kill yeast; it is best to use a thermometer.

**To bake rolls immediately, preheat oven to 375°F. Bake 15 to 20 minutes or until golden brown. Immediately remove from pan. Serve warm.

Step 6. Testing dough to see if it has doubled in bulk.

Step 7. Punching down dough.

Step 8. Shaping dough into rolls.

Challah

2 packages active dry yeast
2 tablespoons sugar
1½ cups water (110° to 115°F)
4 eggs, divided
7 to 7½ cups all-purpose flour, divided
¼ cup butter or margarine, softened
1 teaspoon salt

1. To proof yeast, sprinkle yeast and sugar over warm water in small bowl; stir until yeast is dissolved. Let stand 5 minutes until mixture is bubbly.*

2. To separate 1 egg white from yolk, gently tap egg in center against hard surface, such as side of bowl. Holding shell half in each hand, gently transfer yolk back and forth between 2 shell halves. Allow white to drip down between 2 shells into bowl. When all white has dripped into bowl, place yolk in custard cup; cover with plastic wrap. Reserve yolk in refrigerator.

3. Beat yeast mixture, 2 cups flour, butter and salt in large bowl with electric mixer at low speed, scraping down side of bowl once. Increase mixer speed to medium; beat 2 minutes. Beat in egg white, 3 whole eggs and 1¼ cups flour with electric mixer at low speed, scraping down side of bowl once. Increase mixer speed to medium; beat 2 minutes.

4. Stir in enough additional flour (about 2½ cups) with wooden spoon to make a soft dough.

5. Turn dough out onto well floured surface; flatten slightly. To knead dough, fold dough in half toward you and press dough away from you with heels of hands. Give dough a quarter turn and continue folding, pushing and turning. Continue kneading 5 minutes or until smooth and elastic, adding more flour to prevent sticking, if necessary.

continued on page 90

Step 1. Proofing yeast.

Step 2. Separating an egg white from an egg yolk.

Step 5. Kneading dough.

Challah, continued

6. Shape dough into ball; place in large greased bowl. Turn dough over so that top is greased. Cover with clean kitchen towel. Let rise in warm place (80° to 85°F) away from drafts about 1½ hours or until doubled in bulk.

7. To test dough, lightly press 2 fingertips about ½ inch into dough. Dough is ready if indentations remain when fingertips are removed.

8. Punch down dough by pushing down the center of dough with fist, then pushing edges of dough into center. Turn dough onto lightly floured surface. Knead dough several turns to remove all of the large air bubbles; cover with towel for 15 minutes to let dough rest. Grease 1 large cookie sheet.

9. To prepare dough to be braided, divide dough into 3 pieces. Cut one piece into thirds. Roll each third into 16-inch-long rope using hands.

10. Place ropes side by side and braid; pinch both ends to seal and place on prepared baking sheet for bottom part of loaf.

11. Repeat with another dough piece for another loaf, placing braids at least 5 inches apart on cookie sheet.

12. For top parts of loaves, cut remaining piece of dough in half; cut each half into thirds. Roll each third into 17-inch-long rope using hands. Place ropes side by side and braid; pinch both ends to seal. Carefully place small braid on a braid on baking sheet, stretching top braid if necessary. Tuck ends of top braid under bottom braid. Repeat with remaining dough.

13. Cover with clean kitchen towel. Let rise in warm place away from drafts about 1 hour or until doubled in bulk.

14. Preheat oven to 375°F. Beat 1 tablespoon water into reserved egg yolk. Brush top and sides of each loaf with egg mixture.

15. Bake 35 minutes or until bread is browned and loaves sound hollow when tapped with finger. Remove immediately from baking sheet and cool completely on wire racks.

Makes 2 loaves

*If yeast does not bubble, it is no longer active. Discard mixture and start over with new yeast. Always check expiration date on yeast package. Also, water that is too hot will kill yeast; it is best to use a thermometer.

Step 9. Rolling dough into 16-inch-long rope.

Step 10. Braiding dough.

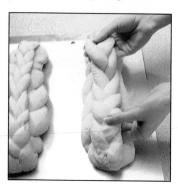

Step 12. Placing small braid over large braid.

Sesame-Onion Twists

2 tablespoons butter or margarine
1½ cups finely chopped onions (technique on page 60)
¼ teaspoon paprika
Nonstick cooking spray
1 loaf (16 ounces) frozen bread dough, thawed*
1 egg, beaten
1 tablespoon sesame seeds

*To thaw frozen bread dough, place frozen loaf in greased 9×5-inch loaf dish, turning loaf over so that top is greased. Cover with plastic wrap. Let stand at room temperature about 4 to 5 hours or until thawed. Or, place frozen bread loaf in plastic bag and refrigerate overnight until thawed.

1. Grease large baking sheet; set aside.

2. Melt butter in medium skillet over medium heat until foamy. Add onions and paprika; cook until onions are tender, stirring occasionally. Remove from heat.

3. Spray work surface, such as countertop or cutting board, with cooking spray. Roll thawed bread dough into 14×12-inch rectangle. If dough gets too elastic or tight, stop rolling dough and let dough rest. It may be necessary to let dough rest several times when rolling dough into a rectangle.

4. Spread onion mixture on one side of dough, making 14×6-inch rectangle. Fold dough over onion mixture to make 14×6-inch rectangle.

5. Pinch 14-inch side of dough to seal. Cut dough into 14 strips, each 6×1 inches.

6. Gently twist a strip 2 times and place on prepared sheet. Press both ends of strip down on cookie sheet. Repeat with remaining strips.

7. Cover with towel. Let twists rise in warm place away from drafts about 40 minutes or until doubled in bulk. Brush with egg, sprinkle with sesame seeds.

8. Preheat oven to 375°F.

9. Bake 15 to 18 minutes or until golden brown. Serve immediately.

Makes 14 bread twists

Step 4. Spreading onion mixture over half of the dough.

Step 5. Cutting dough into 6×1-inch strips.

Step 6. Twisting strips.

INDEX